DC-3 AND C-47
GOONEY BIRDS

Michael O'Leary

Motorbooks International
Publishers & Wholesalers ®

First published in 1992 by Motorbooks International Publishers & Wholesalers, PO Box 2, 729 Prospect Avenue, Osceola, WI 54020 USA

Library of Congress Cataloging-in-Publication Data
O'Leary, Michael (Michael D.)
    DC-3 and C-47 gooney birds / Michael O'Leary.
        p.   cm.
    Includes index.
    ISBN 0-87938-543-X
    1. Douglas DC-3 (Transport plane)—History.   2. Douglas DC-3 (Transport plane) I. Title.
TL686.D65064   1992
628.133'340423—dc20   92-13049

Printed in Hong Kong

On the front cover: Two Gooney Birds operated by the Otis Spunkmeyer chocolate chip cookie company in San Francisco. The aircraft in the foreground was delivered to the US Army Air Corps in October 1938 as a C-41, the first military Gooney. N97H in the background was delivered to the US Army Air Forces in 1945 as a C-47B.

On the back cover: *Upper left*, this brightly painted Gooney was operated by the US Bureau of Land Management in Alaska. *Lower left*, the B-23 Dragon was a bomber variant of the DC-3. *Upper right*, a Canadian Forces Dakota painted in the World War II markings of No. 437 Squadron. *Lower right*, a Canadian Forces Dakota shortly before the type was retired in 1989.

Contents

Two's on First

With the DC-2, Donald Douglas paved the way for a radical change in commercial aviation.

When a Transcontinental and Western Airlines (TWA) Fokker F-10A tri-motor airliner plunged to earth with fatal results on 31 March 1931 after the wooden wing failed in flight, the emerging airlines in the United States knew it was time for a drastic change in airliner design. Previously, airliners had been rather stately Edwardian affairs that made considerable use of wooden structures and fabric covering. Usually droning through the air at under 100 miles per hour, these aircraft offered sometimes unpredictable service—especially if heavy weather was present along the planned flight route. Passengers on these machines needed a sense of adventure.

America's Bureau of Air Commerce quickly followed the Fokker crash, which killed football hero Knute Rockne, with a directive to conduct frequent and costly

The pilot and copilot positions in the DC-2 offer adequate, but not great, visibility and, as can be seen in this view, upward visibility is not particularly good. The legend "U.S. Mail A.M. 2" means that the airline had secured Air Mail Route 2 from the government and used the craft to carry mail along with the passengers. These air mail contracts were extremely important to the early airlines since they brought in much needed cash and often spelled the difference between profit and loss.

inspections of the airlines' wooden-winged aircraft. Since most airlines were barely on the fringe of being profitable, the new directive obviously spelled the end for airliners of wooden construction. Two major problems remained: Where would the new generation of airliners come from, and how would they be funded?

In Seattle, Boeing was working on a new all-metal machine with retractable landing gear that promised excellent performance while completely avoiding the new inspection decree since there was not one splinter of wood to be found in the design. TWA looked to Boeing with some hope but was rudely informed that TWA would have to get in line and wait until a United Airlines order for sixty Boeing Model 247s was fulfilled before they would be able to obtain the new machine. This was not an unnatural response from Boeing since the airframe manufacturer was owned by a consortium that also included United Airlines among its businesses!

The Boeing rebuff did, however, leave TWA in a quandary since United was TWA's main rival and the introduction of a new United airliner along with the attendant bad publicity from the Fokker crash could well put TWA out of business.

At Santa Monica, California's, Clover Field, Jack Frye, the then vice president in charge of operations at Douglas Aircraft

Company, made a bold move and approached TWA with an innovative plan. Since the world of aviation was, at the time, quite small, Frye knew TWA was in trouble and Douglas wanted to establish itself in the world of commercial aviation. So what could be more natural than to combine forces and create a new airliner that would not only save TWA but establish Douglas in the forefront of commercial aircraft development?

After initial contacts had been made, TWA specified they desired an all-metal *tri*-motor airliner. Airlines of the time thought that three engines equated safety—a false hope, since few tri-motors would hold altitude with just two engines operating. Correspondence went back and forth and with the availability of new, more powerful radial engines, Douglas was able to convince TWA that a modern twin-engine aircraft would more than meet the airline's demands. TWA did not keep an exclusive agreement with Douglas and the proposal for a new airliner was spread among the majority of American aircraft companies—all hungry for new orders in the extremely lean years of the Great Depression.

Douglas and Frye envisioned a design that would carry a minimum of twelve passengers and two pilots. Other requirements included a range of at least 1,080 miles, a top speed of 185 miles per hour with a cruise speed of 150 miles per hour, and

Previous page
With a characteristic belch of smoke, the Wright SGR-1820-F52 bursts into life as Douglas DC-2-118B NC1934D (construction number 1368) and prepares for a flight from Santa Monica, California's, Clover Field— where the plane was built and delivered to Pan American World Airways on 16 March 1935. After a couple of years' service with Pan Am, the DC-2 was transferred to Mexicana, *which was controlled by Pan Am, and was given the Mexican registration XA-BJL. The DC-2 was later sold to* Aviateca *in Guatemala as LG-ACA (later changed to TG-ACA) on 28 November 1940. It flew with that carrier until the early 1950s.*

a gross weight of no more than 14,200 pounds. A low landing speed of no more than 65 miles per hour was also desired along with an initial rate of climb of 1,200 feet per minute. TWA demanded an extremely important performance specification that was worded, "This plane, fully loaded, must make satisfactory takeoffs under good control at any TWA airport on any combination of two engines." Since some of the airline's operating fields were "hot and high," the requirement was difficult at best.

After the TWA specification requirement was sent out on 2 August 1932, Donald Douglas and his talented band of engineers decided to create an aircraft that would best the Boeing 247 in all areas. Fortunately, engine development had proceeded to the point where reliable 700 horsepower units were available, and Douglas drew up a fairly

The DC-1 and DC-2 were some of the very first commercial aircraft to benefit from the use of a wind tunnel, and the DC-2 is positively sleek in a refined Art Deco manner when compared to the lumbering Fokker and Ford tri-motors that the Douglas transport replaced. The DC-2's distinctive swept-back outer wing panels span an even eighty-five feet.

sleek design that included a multi-spar wing (courtesy of John K. Northrop who, at the time, was employed at Douglas) that would give the aircraft great strength. The wing center section would be built integral with the fuselage, eliminating the annoying spar such as that on the 247 which ran through the cabin and caused difficulty for passengers and crew alike.

The only other airworthy DC-2 is construction number 1404, which was delivered to the US Navy as an R2D-1, Bureau of Aeronautics serial number (BuNo) 9993, at Naval Air Station (NAS) Anacostia, Washington, DC, on 7 September 1935 where it served as a transport for ranking officers. The aircraft flew through most of World War II until it was withdrawn from service on 28 August 1944. After the war, the plane was sold surplus as NC39165 and went through several owners including Mercer Airlines before being sold to Colgate Darden III of Cayce, South Carolina, in September 1968. Colgate finished the aircraft in General Air Lines markings and operated the plane infrequently. In 1983, the aircraft was leased by KLM and painted in the markings of PH-AJU, the KLM transport that came in second (carrying some paying passengers and mail) in the October 1934 MacRoberston Race from England to Australia, only being beaten by a specially designed de Havilland Comet racer. The DC-2 re-created the race and garnered much publicity for KLM. This aircraft is seldom flown.

On 12 August, Harry Wetzel and Arthur Raymond went to TWA in New York to present the Douglas proposal, which was called the DC-1 for Douglas Commercial One. It was not an easy sell—TWA was extremely concerned that the DC-1 meet its tough requirement and negotiations continued for three weeks.

A deal was finally hammered out that saw a contract signed in which TWA would pay $125,000 for the prototype aircraft with an option to purchase all or some of the first lot of sixty aircraft for a unit price of $58,000, minus engines and propellers. At this time, General Motors Corporation had a controlling interest in TWA and owned a company called General Aviation (later to become North American Aviation) so, in case the DC-1 did not live up to expectations, General Motors instructed General Aviation to proceed on the design and construction of a tri-motor aircraft that could be put into service.

With the contract signed, Douglas got busy on detail design work. As with virtually every aircraft design through history, it was

soon obvious that the DC-1 would weigh more than originally planned. The contract to supply engines for the aircraft was hotly contested between Wright and Pratt & Whitney. Douglas initially picked the Wright SGR-1820-F radial engine of 690 horsepower, fitted with Hamilton Standard three-blade, variable-pitch propellers. The creation of a workable variable-pitch prop went a long way in helping the DC-1 meet the strict engine-out requirement.

Unlike today's aircraft which often take years to create after the signing of a contract, the DC-1 was ready in a mere nine months—and these nine months included such then-revolutionary testing methods as the use of a wind tunnel and building of a full-size fuselage mockup. On 1 July 1933, the aircraft, carrying the experimental registration X223Y, lifted off from Clover Field with Carl Cover and Fred Herman as pilots. First flights are always fraught with doubt and when Cover and Herman reached cruising altitude, both engines suddenly quit! It was only due to the skill of the crew that the plane was saved and, by dropping to a lower altitude, the crew managed to get the powerplants restarted and safely returned to Clover Field. The problem was traced to a fuel line fault.

Flight testing continued but it was not without problems—including a belly landing after the pilots forgot to put the gear down. For two months the aircraft was flown by pilots from Douglas and TWA for intensive evaluation, and the culmination of the testing came on 4 September 1933 when the aircraft flew successfully from Winslow, Arizona, to Albuquerque, New Mexico, with one of the Wrights shut down. The results made TWA happy and a contract was initiated for twenty new DC-2s, the improved production variant of the DC-1.

The DC-1 was to remain a unique aircraft but after securing the TWA contract the plane went on to serve as a flying test bed, cross-country record breaker, and eventually wound up in Spain flying with *Lineas Aereas Postales Espanolas* in support of Spain's Republican government during that country's devastating civil war. During December 1940, the aircraft was written off following an engine failure on takeoff but no one aboard was injured. It is rumored that part of the wreckage was later dragged away and converted into a local religious shrine. The DC-1 had truly paved the way for modern aviation.

TWA's order for twenty new DC-2s also saw a number of changes in the basic design, including the lengthening of the fuselage by two feet in order to increase the number of passenger seats to fourteen and the addition of Wright SGR-1820-F3 Cyclone radials of increased horsepower. TWA was eager to press the aircraft into service. The first production model, registered NC13711, lifted off from Santa Monica on 11 May 1934—by which time production was in full swing.

The aviation community quickly realized that Douglas had a world-beater and international interest in the type resulted in license rights being issued to Fokker in The Netherlands and Nakajima Hikoki in Japan.

The vertical tail of the DC-2 is greatly different from the DC-3, an example of which can be seen in the background. The tail carries the famous Douglas logo "First Around the World," which commemorates the fact that in 1924 the four Douglas World Cruisers became the first aircraft to circumnavigate the globe. The DC-2 stands sixteen feet three and three-quarters inches high.

As it turned out, Fokker did not build any DC-2s but did sell quite a few of the aircraft while the Japanese did set up a production line and built five aircraft for Greater Japan Air Lines.

Douglas had invested heavily with the DC-1 and the TWA contract price covered only about one third of the aircraft's total cost. However, the DC-2 was a great success for the company and they broke even after fifty DC-2s had been built. Douglas built 193 DC-2s in three civil and eight military variants and, of the civil operators, TWA was the largest, eventually ordering thirty-one aircraft. Other operators of new-built DC-2s included General Air Lines, Panagra, Eastern Air Lines, American Airlines, and Pan American. TWA immediately put its first aircraft on the Columbus-Pittsburgh-Newark route on 18 May 1934. As more aircraft became available, they began adding DC-2s

Previous page
This view of NC1934D illustrates the glowing polished aluminum skin of the craft— evidence of the care lavished on it by the Douglas Historical Foundation in their long battle to restore the transport and keep it flying.

to their most popular routes including a transcontinental flight from New York to Grand Central Air Terminal, Glendale, California, which, at the time, was the main airline hub for Los Angeles. The DC-2 was able to fly from Glendale to New York in just over sixteen hours and TWA immediately captured the transcontinental business from United and its slower and less comfortable Boeing 247s.

From the beginning, the DC-2 was a hard-working moneymaker and the plane put Douglas on the aeronautical map. Over the years, DC-2s covered the world and as the planes were phased out of service with the large airlines, many found their way to Third World countries where they began to establish air routes. During World War II, many DC-2s were drafted into military service to join the various military variants of the craft. With such hard service under its wings, it is not surprising that the number of surviving DC-2s rapidly dwindled due to accidents, retirement, and enemy action. Today, just two DC-2s remain flyable, and the accompanying photographs illustrate what is probably the better known of the two.

NC14271 was originally delivered to Pan American World Airways during March 1935, and it immediately went into service.

The stately lines of the DC-2 in flight illustrate the sweep back to the outer wing panels. The use of a multi-spar wing design created a wing of exceptional strength that helped give the DC-2 and DC-3 series a virtually unlimited airframe life.

After a couple of years, NC14271 was transferred to Pan American's Mexican affiliate, *Mexicana,* in October 1937, and the plane began flying the skies over the vast and dusty nation. The rugged transport was particularly valuable in Third World countries where up-to-date maintenance and repair facilities were not always readily available.

The DC-2's next step was to join *Avianca* in Guatemala during October 1940 where it led a long and hard life as a jack-of-all-trades transport, finally being sold off in June 1953. The new owner was the Johnson Flying Service, operators of a large eclectic collection of veteran and vintage aircraft that were worked hard on a variety of tasks. Flown to the company's main base at Missoula, Montana, the plane was modified for aerial spraying with the addition of an internal fuselage tank for pesticides and spray bars under the wings. The aircraft was also used for carrying and dropping smoke jumpers.

13

Out over the Pacific, N1934D displays an airline paint scheme that it never wore. The Douglas Historical Foundation decided to paint the aircraft in Transcontinental and Western Airlines (TWA) markings since that was the first airline to operate the type. In order to capitalize on the worldwide fame of Charles Lindbergh, TWA made the pioneer aviator a lucrative offer in order to prominently display his name on their aircraft. As war clouds gathered in Europe and Lindbergh's pro-German statements became more controversial, plans for the use of "The Lindberg Line" were quietly dropped by the company.

Johnson Flying Service also operated several Ford Tri-Motors in the smoke jumper role so the DC-2, now registered N4867V, was in the company of transports of even greater vintage. It flew in a hazardous new trade as the aircraft fought currents of super-heated firestorm air while dropping the daring smoke jumpers near the perimeters of huge forest fires.

Rather amazingly, N4867V survived its harsh battles with nature until 1973 when the plane was traded to Stan Burnstein as partial payment for a used Douglas DC-8 with which Johnson started a (disastrous) airline venture. Burnstein, in turn, decided to donate the

transport to the Donald Douglas Museum and Library at Clover Field, the aircraft's birthplace.

The museum, a private group of enthusiasts, was underfunded and the bare-metal DC-2 soon began to look rather shabby in Clover Field's salt-laden environment. In July 1982, the Douglas Historical Foundation was created by the Douglas Aircraft Company Management Club to take over the plane and restore the machine to its former glory. It was not an easy task—the DC-2 had been a workhorse for its entire career and it showed. Volunteers set to work and, over the

years, tens of thousands of man-hours were spent bringing the aircraft back to its original condition.

The interior was gutted when received, but seats were tracked down and the original fabrics and colors were duplicated. The airframe was thoroughly overhauled, fresh engines fitted, and all wiring restored. It was a big task but it was also a task aided by many of the subcontractors who have supplied Douglas for many years.

On 25 April 1987—fourteen years after it had last flown—the DC-2 once again took to the air from Long Beach Airport. The aircraft was a masterpiece of the restorer's art, gleaming in polished metal finish. Like most vintage aircraft, however, the restored transport had its share of mechanical

problems. Several failed engines caused trouble with air show schedules and caused the restorers to dip deeply into their limited funds. During this period, the Douglas Museum was purchased by David Price and turned into his well-funded, high-tech Museum of Flying which opened its doors in 1989. Currently, the DC-2 is on lease to the Douglas Historical Foundation and when the lease expires, the plane will go to the Museum of Flying and will be kept operational.

Until that time, the DC-2 flies on and on, visiting air shows and other aeronautical events to remind the general public of the aircraft that paved the way for the DC-3 and made America dominant in the field of commercial aviation.

The rather flat sides of the sixty-one foot eleven and three-quarters inch fuselage is emphasized in this rear view of DC-2 N1934D in flight. The fuselage of the DC-3 is much more rounded. When obtained by Johnson Flying Service in 1953, the interior was stripped and R-1820-52B engines were installed. A large insecticide tank was installed in the fuselage and spray bars were fitted under the wings. The plane was used for large-acreage spraying but during the fire season, the tank was removed and the DC-2 was used to drop smoke jumpers. During its service with Johnson, the craft was registered N4867V.

airplanes to be delivered on this order or if in its opinion first airplane is materially depreciated account development testing or revisions. Price $79,500 each complete except for radio, automatic pilot and engines." At this point, the groundwork for aviation history was being established. Douglas replied on 9 July, "Accept your order for ten

Previous page
Gear fully down, N711Y heads back for Burbank Airport. Note the window added to the flight deck for better visibility. Shortly after these photographs were taken, N711Y plunged to earth in flames near De Kalb, Texas, killing singer Rick Nelson and six members of his entourage. Although badly burned, both pilots survived. The accident was later traced to a faulty cabin heater that was fueled with avgas.

DST airplanes in accordance with your telegram 8 July."

Wright promised their upgraded radial would deliver 1,000 horsepower, and Littlewood's drawings and calculations, after conference with Douglas, estimated eighty percent of the DC-2's parts could be used on the DST. Unfortunately, as with most optimistic aircraft projects, it turned out that the "Super DC-2" would never exist. The new aircraft, Douglas Commercial Three (DC-3), was a product of lots of hard work between the two companies but, in the end, the DC-3 had only about ten percent of its parts compatible with the earlier DC-2. The DC-3 was basically an entirely new aircraft that sort of looked like the DC-2 but was bigger all the way around, had more power, and was much stronger.

The team that did the detail design work on the DC-3 was led by Arthur Raymond. Lee Atwood (who would later significantly

C-47A-75-DL USAAF serial number 42-100828 was built at Long Beach and began operations with the Eighth Air Force on 6 March 1944. It probably served during the D-day invasion. After USAAF service, the aircraft was placed in storage in West Germany and then given to Norway on 20 November 1950 as part of the US military Defense Assistance Program. During Norwegian service, the craft flew with No. 335 Squadron and was transferred to Denmark on 20 September 1956 where it took up the markings K-685. The Danish aircraft were kept in beautiful condition, and this plane even appeared in the movie A Bridge Too Far. *During October 1982, the plane was one of three C-47s sold to the Valiant Air Command (VAC) in Titusville, Florida. In this view K-685, now registered N3240T, is seen dropping a load of skydivers during the VAC's annual air show, while being accompanied by a de Havilland Beaver.*

19

This beautifully restored R4D-6-DK is owned and operated by the Mid-Atlantic Air Museum in Pennsylvania. BuNo 50819 was assigned to Fleet Air Wing 5, Norfolk, Virginia, in January 1945 and flew with a number of Naval Air Transport Service (NATS) units. Toward the end of its service life, the plane was converted to an R4D-6S with antisubmarine warfare (ASW) gear. During the late 1950s, the plane received a civil registration of N9119Z, then changed to N60 and operated with the US Navy. In 1959, the craft went into storage at NAS Litchfield Park, Arizona. It came alive again as N60 (then to N68) with the Federal Aviation

Administration during 1966, one of over sixty such aircraft transferred to the FAA. The plane went through several other governmental agencies including the Department of Agriculture before going into storage once again. On 2 June 1981, the craft was purchased, as N229GB, by the Mid-Atlantic Air Museum and restored to impeccable NATS configuration by the museum's volunteers. In 1982, the R4D won Best Transport Award at the annual Experimental Aircraft Association (EAA) Convention in Oshkosh, Wisconsin. During 1983, the plane became more upscale and won the EAA's Grand Champion Award.

contribute to the P-51) was responsible for stress analysis, and Ed Burton supervised basic layout. Dr. Bailey Oswald was in charge of aerodynamics. This talented team helped rush through the development of the DC-3 in order that construction of prototype NC14988 could begin during December 1934—while major negotiations were still being undertaken between the two major parties!

It took just one year to complete the first aircraft and NC14988 went aloft on 17 December 1935 from Clover Field with Carl Cover, Frank Collbohm, and Ed Stineman comprising the flight test crew. Fortunately, flight testing of the DC-3/DST went smoothly

and by the end of the month, the plane had logged nearly twenty-six hours of flying time accrued during twenty-six flights. During this time, Dan Beard, the engineering test pilot for American, also undertook some of the flying so that he could report directly back to Smith.

Douglas had studied the popular pullman railway cars then in use and adapted some of their features to the interior, including the use of pleasing colors that would allow passengers to relax and give them a feeling of spaciousness. Also, a private compartment was fitted in the forward fuselage and two separate lavatories were installed. The cabin was well-insulated to reduce noise while convenient vents were provided throughout the cabin to allow the interior air to change once per minute (remember, this was before pressurized aircraft).

A major problem occurred during test flights when it was realized that it was taking more than 1,000 feet to become airborne. Because of this, TWA (another interested observer) decided not to order the new DC-3 and, instead, placed an order for more DC-2s, which they knew could safely operate out of some of their smaller fields. The engines were taken apart by Douglas and Wright engineers, and they found an oil blockage that was probably dropping about seventy-five horsepower from each engine. A simple fix was required and the engines were placed back on the prototype. During the next flight, the DC-3 got airborne in under 1,000 feet and the requirement was satisfied. TWA attempted to reinstate its order but the company's production slots had been taken over by American and United. So TWA would not get its first DC-3 until over two dozen were flying with the other airlines.

The past meets the present. During May 1981, a DC-3 belonging to Britain's Eastern Airways (now defunct) was displayed with a British Airways Concorde doublesonic transport to show what a difference a few decades make. Oddly, the DC-3 will probably long outfly the limited-production Concorde.

The DC-3/DST immediately grabbed the attention of all major airlines and American generously used its prototype to give demonstration flights to officials from rival airlines. They liked what they saw and the orders started to pour into Douglas.

American formally accepted its first DST on 29 April 1936 and started its Flagship service the following month with *Flagship Illinois* at Chicago and *Flagship New York* at Newark, New Jersey. Douglas anticipated only a small run of aircraft—perhaps up to

Provincetown-Boston Airlines/Naples Airlines bought DC-3s during January 1968 to replace their aging Lockheed 10 Electras on commuter flights. At one time, the airline was operating at least a dozen DC-3s. N33PB (ex-N233PB) was built as a C-53-DO Skytrooper at Oklahoma City and delivered to the USAAF on 22 May 1942 as serial number 42-6942. After operating in North Africa, the plane was brought back to the States and assigned to Pan American on 6 August 1944. Just five days later the craft was with Mid-Continent Air Lines as NC34952, and they operated the transport until sale to Braniff Airlines, as a DC-3-SIC3G, on 15 August 1952. On 1 December 1959, it was sold to Trans-Texas Airways, and after a few years of service went on to several other operators until sold to Provincetown-Boston Airways in 1968. On 25 May 1986, the aircraft was registered as YV-427C in Caracas, Venezuela, and remains active in that country.

one-hundred—and the company was somewhat reluctant to order more material for construction. Little did Donald Douglas realize the future of the DC-3.

American was very happy with its nonstop New York–to–Chicago service and gained considerable publicity from the fact that it only took three hours fifty-five minutes to fly east (the train took eighteen hours). The planes were extremely economical to operate, meaning that American could make a profit on passengers—and not just on the mail.

By July 1937 Douglas stopped DC-2 production to concentrate on the DC-3/DST. At the end of 1936, American had taken delivery of seven DSTs and thirteen DC-3s. Although the DST was a novel yet effective concept, more profit could be made with the DC-3's greater seating capacity. Export

Basking in a pastoral Caribbean setting, Air British Virgin Islands (BVI) VP-LVK is finished in an attractive paint scheme. Operating from Tortola, British Virgin Islands, the company flew a small fleet of Gooney Birds on scheduled inter-island services. VP-LVK was originally built as C-47-DL serial number 41-38671 and delivered to the USAAF on 29 November 1942. Sold shortly after the war, the plane went through many owners and registrations including NC75410, N5117, and N5117X. In November 1976, the craft went to Air BVI where it became VP-LVK. Stephen Piercey

The Gooney Bird has become a fairly uncommon sight in Great Britain, but thanks to Air Atlantique, the type does keep showing up in British skies. Formed in 1977 and operating out of Coventry and Jersey, the company does charter work with its DC-3. They also attend air shows and give rides. The company is the largest DC-3 operator in the United Kingdom and has around a half dozen operating DC-3s and two DC-6s. Some of the DC-3s have been modified for antipollution work under a contract to the British government. G-AMPO was delivered to the Royal Air Force (RAF) on 5 May 1945 as KN566 and operated at many different stations until being sold surplus in 1948. The plane operated with several charter outfits including Starways Limited and Eastern Airways until passing to Air Atlantique ownership on 21 October 1981. Stephen Piercey

orders soon started coming in, and Fokker was appointed the European representative, while licensing agreements were reached with Russia and Japan.

The majority of orders were for the DC-3, and the DST was a luxury at a time airlines were looking for hard-found profit. Seating was eventually increased to a twenty-eight-passenger configuration—twice the capacity of the DC-2. The effect of the DC-3 can easily be gauged as it rapidly began replacing less efficient airliners: There were 460 passenger aircraft in US service during 1935 but by 1940, the number had decreased to 358 aircraft—and most were DC-3s. Even though the overall number of planes had reduced, the passenger-carried figure had more than quadrupled.

Each airline had its own interior and equipment specifications for their DC-3s, and a number of variants were built, including the DC-3B powered by Wright Cyclone SGR-1820-G202A radials of 1,200 horsepower each. Eastern, United, and

American were all flying DC-3s by 1937 and foreign sales were increasing. By 1939, however, the war in Europe put an end to Fokker's selling campaign and the majority of aircraft were taken over by the air forces of the nations in which they operated.

At the Santa Monica factory, production was brisk. War clouds were on the horizon, and Douglas was receiving military orders for a variety of warplanes. By the time of Pearl Harbor, Douglas had built 266 DC-3s, 114 DC-3As, ten DC-3Bs, twenty-one DSTs, and nineteen DST-As. Contracts had been received for 149 more aircraft and these were immediately confiscated by the military. Many DC-3s in airline service were also taken over by the military and given a bewildering variety of designations that included C-48, C-49, C-50, C-52, C-53, and C-68.

The Army Air Corps already had military variants of the DC-2 in operation so it was only natural that their interest would turn to the DC-3. The first military variant of

the DC-3, the unique C-41, was ordered on 17 August 1939, and became the personal transport for Gen. H. H. "Hap" Arnold. Amazingly, this historic aircraft has survived and is still flying, as discussed in another chapter.

With the war, Douglas was flooded with contracts and it was impossible to build all the aircraft the military wanted at Santa Monica. The new military variant was to be designated C-47 and it would be an aircraft that would earn a proud place in combat history. The first contract for C-47s was awarded on 16 September 1940, during the height of the Battle of Britain. These aircraft would be constructed at the new Douglas plant in nearby Long Beach. Because of the increasing demand, another C-47 factory was opened at Oklahoma City, Oklahoma, and the overwhelming process of American mass production was set to begin.

The first C-47s were given the appropriate name of Skytrain, and the plane differed from the DC-3 in that it had a large two-panel cargo door on the left side of the fuselage, reinforced floor with tie-downs to handle heavy military equipment such as jeeps or artillery pieces, military-style seating arrangements, an astrodome, military electronics, and a slightly revised fuel system. With a three-man flight crew, the aircraft could haul twenty-eight airborne troops, fourteen stretchers, or 6,000 pounds of cargo.

As the aircraft began to pour into US Army Air Forces (USAAF) service (the service's name was changed in 1942), the military found they did not have an efficient transport aircraft system in place nor did they have enough crews for the planes. Accordingly, many airline crews were pressed into service to fly the aircraft as well as to instruct upcoming generations of C-47 pilots and mechanics. It was a frantic time at best, and after Pearl Harbor emergency C-47 missions were undertaken to supply areas that the Army feared would come under enemy attack—such as the west coast of the United States and the Panama Canal Zone.

New air links had to be forged to Britain to ensure an increasing flow of war supplies to American forces and the Allies. With very

Over the years, the FAA (and the earlier Civil Aeronautics Authority [CAA]) operated a large fleet of DC-3s to accomplish a wide variety of tasks including airways calibration. Painted in their distinctive colors, the aircraft were a common sight during the 1960s and 1970s at airports around the country. These two examples, N33 and N35, are seen on 1 December 1981 at Oklahoma City. N33 was originally built as R4D-6-DK BuNo 50793 and delivered to the Navy during November 1944. Acquired as N33 by the CAA in 1956 (becoming FAA in 1966), the registration was canceled during 1982, and the plane transferred to the Minnesota Air National Guard Museum where it is now on display. N35 was built as R4D-6-DK BuNo 39098 and operated extensively in the Pacific. It eventually went into storage at NAS Litchfield Park before being acquired by the CAA in 1966. After being phased out of FAA service in 1982, the plane was placed on static display at Pope Air Force Base (AFB) in North Carolina until 1982. Charles E. Stewart

Many surplus FAA DC-3s continued their flying careers after being sold surplus. One of over sixty R4Ds acquired by the CAA/FAA, N69 originally began life as BuNo 17286 and then went to the CAA as N62, but this was changed to N69 in 1973. After being disposed of by the FAA in the early 1980s, the plane was purchased by an aircraft dealer, refurbished, registered N259DC, and painted in Brazilian national colors. The Gooney is seen during August 1988 as it departs Chino, California, on its way to a new home in the Brazilian aerospace museum.

little in the way of maps or navigation aids, brave crews from Northeast Airlines developed the soon-to-be-famous aerial route that would link America from Britain via Presque Isle, Maine, to Prestwick, Scotland. The C-47s pioneered the way for massive flights of bombers, fighters, and transports that were pouring off American production lines.

In order to create a central transport service, the USAAF established the Air Transport Command (ATC) on 20 June 1942, and as aircraft and personnel accumulated, the ATC was soon staging operations in many parts of the world. The Gooney Bird, as the C-47 was nicknamed by military troops after a Pacific island bird incapable of sustained flight, began to forge a history of legendary deeds in diverse and hostile parts of the globe. Although the World War II exploits of the aircraft would fill several volumes, they are outside the scope of this book, but it should be noted that Gen. Dwight D. Eisenhower stated that the C-47 was one of the ten reasons the Allies won the war.

C-47s were also supplied to the Allies (and called Dakota in Commonwealth service) and, by the end of the war, the C-47

was literally operating from every Allied location on the globe. Also, the Navy and Marines were flying large numbers of Goonies under the designation R4D.

Japan, which had purchased license rights to the DC-3 before the war, made its own military variant called the L2D and went on to build almost 500 examples. These aircraft were occasionally encountered by American fighter pilots and attacked only after the pilots made sure the aircraft was carrying the *hinomaru* national insignia.

Russia, also a license holder, went on to build over 2,000 examples called Li-2s and PS-84s. These aircraft served well during the war and operated for many years afterward with the Soviets and their allies. The Soviet Union was also supplied with Lend-Lease C-47s from American factories.

Santa Monica, Long Beach, and Oklahoma City went on to build an amazing total of 10,654 DC-3 and C-47 variants between 1935 and 1947. The success of the type was well beyond the wildest dreams of Douglas. The aircraft had left a permanent stamp on the face of the globe—efficient and reliable aerial transportation was now available on a worldwide scale.

After the war, the Reconstruction Finance Corporation (RFC) sold off hundreds of surplus C-47s, and the surviving DC-3s were returned to their original airline owners. Thriving businesses were set up that converted C-47s to DC-3 configuration while dozens of new nonscheduled airlines cropped up in the United States. Nicknamed "non-scheds" and usually operated by former servicemen, these little airlines would haul anything, anywhere and soon became a thorn in the side of the major airlines that eventually pulled enough political clout to have the majority of the non-scheds knocked out of business for a variety of bureaucratic infractions.

America's allies and many Third World nations were supplied with surplus C-47s as part of a military defense aid package.

Many modifications to improve the Gooney Bird's performance were offered by aeronautical concerns. Several firms

N101KC is typical of the hard-working Gooney Birds that still fly regularly. Built as C-47A-60-DL serial number 42-68712, the plane operated with the Eighth Air Force in Europe during the war. Purchased by Pan American and registered NC45375 on 1 August 1949, the plane was sold in 1956 to a company that had an executive interior installed. Over the years, the plane went through a number of different owners including small airlines like Hawkeye Airlines and Royal West Airline, but was finally abandoned in Thermopolis, Wyoming, in 1977. During 1981, the aircraft was once again made airworthy. In 1987 it was purchased by Ken Spiva who has since been flying the plane as a skydiver platform from Lodi, California, and Coolidge, Arizona, where it was photographed during February 1990.

Latin America has been a huge operator of the DC-3 and C-47—both in the civilian and military role. Over the years, hundreds of the aircraft have ventured "south of the border," either being supplied as US military aid or purchased on the open market. The Fuerza Aerea Colombiana *has been one of the larger operators of the type, and around forty examples were obtained, the first in 1944. Cargo doors open wide, FAC 681 is seen undergoing maintenance during February 1975.*

Gooney Birds gravitated to second- and third-line service all over the world, giving sterling service to remote areas that relied on the DC-3 for communication and travel to other parts of the globe. Many other uses were also found for the craft. As mentioned, executive conversions were popular, while some planes were converted to crop dusters or mosquito sprayers—able to cover large swaths of acreage at an appropriate speed. A few Gooney Birds were even converted into fire bombers, while others were used to drop smoke jumpers near remote forest fires. During the 1970s and 1980s, an unfortunate number of Goonies were expended in the drug running role, and it is not uncommon to find wrecked examples in the shallow waters off Florida or near the Latin American nations where they began their illegal flights.

What is the future of the DC-3 and C-47? It is difficult to know, and many factors are involved. The high-quality aviation fuel that the Gooney's radial engines need is becoming difficult to find. There is always a chance the Federal Aviation Administration

Aircraft that operate in Alaska are often painted in bright colors to facilitate sighting in the snow in case they are forced down. N645 was no exception. Delivered to the Navy as R4D-6 BuNo 50779, the craft saw a number of Stateside and Pacific assignments until being surplused as N701 in 1958. The plane went to the Bureau of Land Management in Alaska from June 1965 to April 1977 and then to the US Department of Agriculture as N214GB. From 1980 to 1984, the plane served with the US Forest Service. The aircraft is now painted in military markings and is on display at Maxwell AFB in Alabama in non-airworthy condition. Photographed at Anchorage during July 1973, the red and yellow Gooney is fitted with a jet-assisted takeoff (JATO) bottle under the fuselage.

*The last military user of the North American
P-51 Mustang was* Fuerza Aerea Dominicana.
*The Dominican Republic also operated about
a dozen C-47s, one of which is seen heading
toward a paratrooper drop, escorted by two
P-51Ds during June 1982. It is thought that
several of the C-47s still remain operational
with the country's air arm.*

Certainly one of the most attractive Gooney Birds illustrated in this volume is C-FTDJ, seen flying over Canadian territory during October 1982. C-FTDJ originally started on the Santa Monica production line as a DC-3-454 for the Netherlands East Indies Air Force. This aircraft was pressed into American service before completion with the designation C-49J, serial number 43-1985. The plane remained in the States during its military service and went back to Douglas when sold surplus. The company converted the plane to DC-3-G202A standard and sold the craft to Trans-Canada Airlines as its first DC-3. In 1948, the Gooney was registered to Goodyear Canada Limited, and the company

had the craft converted to executive-transport configuration by Canadair. This modification included changing the Cyclone engines to Twin Wasp powerplants, installing a fourteen-seat interior, and putting panorama windows in the fuselage. Goodyear operated the plane for the rest of its service life, and the aircraft was in magnificent condition when flown on its last flight to the National Aviation Museum in Rockcliffe, Ottawa, on 19 December 1983, where it now permanently resides. Its last flight brought the total number of flying hours up to 22,284—low for a Gooney Bird! Note the fuselage light, which is used to check the engines during night operations. Stephen Piercey

35

South Africa has always been a large user of Gooney Birds, and well over one hundred have served (or continue to serve) in the South African Air Force where the majority have flown combat missions against rebels. The civil scene in South Africa has also seen the operation of about one hundred DC-3s, and many aircraft still remain active. ZS-JMP was originally built as a DC-3-209B for TWA on 16 April 1939 and served with TWA until mid-1950 when it was sold to the Remmert Werner Corporation, which specialized in DC-3 modifications. The company installed Pratt & Whitney Twin Wasps in place of the Cyclones and sold the craft to Minnesota Mining and Manufacturing (3M) as N33M. In 1967, the plane went to Aero Service Corporation, a large survey company, which registered the craft N190UM and added many modifications for its survey role. In 1971, the plane went to South Africa as ZS-JMP and received further heavy modifications for its mission. Operated by Avex Air, the aircraft was also used for spraying tsetse flies in Botswana; this high-angle view shows the many modifications made to the vintage Gooney.

Even in the days of the space age, the National Aeronautics and Space Administration (NASA) found a place for the Gooney Bird. Although they are now all retired, it was not uncommon to see a NASA Gooney at Edwards AFB during early Space Shuttle operations. N817NA was originally delivered as R4D-5 BuNo 17136 on 13 January 1944 and served in the Far East for a number of years before being transferred to NASA as a C-47H during 1964. In 1981, the plane was given to the Golden Triangle Vo-Tech Center in Mississippi but was recently sold to a new owner. N817NA was photographed at Edwards AFB during January 1987.

Its drab Luftwaffe/NATO camouflage accented with a few DaGlo splashes, this aircraft, 14 + 11, was used as an F-104 radar trainer, complete with an F-104 nose, when photographed at Husum, West Germany, during September 1969. Originally delivered on 2 July 1945 to the RAF as KP250, the plane went to the new Luftwaffe during 1955 and was converted to the F-104 trainer in 1963. After being surplused in the early 1970s, the craft was registered N90904 but eventually wound up in South Africa. Its fate is uncertain.

Provincetown-Boston Airlines/Naples Airlines was taken over by Eastern Air Lines as Eastern Express in the early 1980s and operated as a commuter/feeder service. Wearing small Provincetown-Boston Airlines titles by the cockpit window, it is interesting to note that N136PB was originally delivered as DC-3-201 NC18121 to Eastern on 23 October 1937! Used as a C-49G during the war, the aircraft went on to fly with Trans-Texas Airways as a DC-3A after the war. Having logged over 90,000 flying hours, N136PB is thought to be the world's highest-time transport. The plane no longer operates with Eastern because the airline is out of business.

Northeast Airlines of Boston flew DC-3s until 1967 when the type was finally replaced by Convairs, ending the airline's twenty-five-year association with the type. A flawless N19428 awaits its next load of passengers on the Boston ramp. This aircraft operated with United Airlines after the war and was obtained by Northeast on 27 February 1953 and sold during 1967.

Heavily marked with American flags, C-47J BuNo 50775 was serving with the naval attache in Thailand when it was photographed during March 1966. Built as an R4D-6 and delivered on 16 November 1944, the aircraft served with a number of Stateside units during the war and was assigned to the naval attache in Singapore during 1964, before moving on to Thailand. Note all the decals ("zaps") near the rear cargo door of all the squadrons and bases that the plane had visited.

C-47-DL N728G is seen on one of its frequent outings from Troy, Alabama, where it is owned by vintage aircraft collector Wiley Sanders. Built as serial number 41-7860, the plane was soon handed over to Braniff who operated it for the military. In October 1945, the craft was flown to Bush Field, Georgia, where it was taken over by the RFC for sale.

Somewhere along the line, N728G acquired speed cowlings and numerous other modifications including a plush executive interior. Wiley Sanders keeps the aircraft in perfect shape, and the plane in its distinctive paint scheme is often seen at air shows across the country.

Originally built as DC-3-201B NC21729 for Eastern Air Lines, this aircraft was delivered on 17 June 1939 from Santa Monica. Surplused by the airline in 1952, the craft soon had another job flying with North Central Airlines until they disposed of the plane in 1964. It then went through a number of owners before winding up in Canada in 1982 as C-GDAK. The plane was acquired by the Canadian Warplane Heritage in 1983 and attractively painted to represent a Royal Canadian Air Force (RCAF) Dakota that served in Burma during 1944. As an airline variant, the DC-3 still retains its passenger door and Wright Cyclones. With over 81,000 flying hours, this is thought to be the second highest-time Gooney Bird flying.

Nostalgia Air Tours Hawaii—the airline that never was. Formed in 1991 by aeronautical horse trader Ascher Ward for hauling tourists in Hawaii, one Gooney Bird was acquired and configured for the operation but sold "when a better offer came along," and before the plane could be flown to Hawaii. N92578 as originally built in Long Beach as C-47-DL serial number 42-32802 and delivered on 10 February 1943. Staying in the United States for its military career, the aircraft was sold on 17 September 1946 as NC9562H. This particular aircraft has gone through a number of owners, and registrations including N75C, N7503, N1800U, and N1800D. One of the owners was Jungle Aviation & Radio Service. Another was the Missionary Aviation Fellowship. In 1973, the plane went to Bolivia as CP-1020 for the Instituto Linguistico de Verano but was returned to the States in 1981. Dubbed The Blast from the Past, *the aircraft, now registered as a DC-3C-S3C4G, is seen over Southern California on a 15 June 1991 proving flight before going to its new owner.*

Beautifully polished and accented with a red stripe, Gooney N11W is seen on the ramp at Reno, Nevada, during December 1972. Delivered as serial number 43-15730 on 3 May 1944, the aircraft was operated by the Air Transport Command until sold surplus in late 1945 to Braniff as NC59749. In 1949, the plane was again sold and registered as N11W. It then went through several different owners, and when photographed was being operated by Bede Aircraft for hauling their little BD-5 homebuilt jet to air shows. The BD-5 turned out to be a boondoggle, and many investors lost their money. N11W went to Canada in 1975 as C-GRMH to fly with a company called Skyservices. It is not known if the plane is still flying.

Over the years, the Gooney Bird has been used for just about every imaginable task, and this fleet of aircraft at Sacramento's Executive Airport, California, during September 1971, was being used on fog dispersion experiments. The fleet was operated by World Weather out of Midland, Texas, and N19937 was originally built as serial number 41-20105—a C-53—and delivered to the Army on 14 February 1942. During its military service, the aircraft traveled to Britain, Egypt, and Africa. On 13 July 1944, the plane was transferred to United Airlines as Mainliner Bakersfield, with registration NC19937. The aircraft was acquired by World Weather in late 1969.

Certainly one of the more garish Gooney Bird paint schemes, N19932 is named Five Easy Pieces, *apparently to complement its gold camouflage. Delivered on 6 May 1942 as a C-53, the aircraft went surplus to United as NC19932 and then through the usual run of owners over the years but, unusually, the registration stayed the same. When photographed during February 1976, the plane was owned by Luxury Flights Incorporated of Rochester, New York. The aircraft's registration was canceled in September 1982 for reasons unknown.*

TC-47B-30-DK serial number 44-76716 was originally delivered to the USAAF during April 1945, but little is known of its history until acquired by the University of Michigan during 1970 as N8704. In 1982, the Gooney was obtained by the Yankee Air Force Museum in Ypsilanti, Michigan. Volunteers at the museum restored the plane back to pristine 1950s condition, and it is regularly flown to air shows. Bill Dodds is seen flying N8704 near Geneseo, New York, during August 1989.

One of the biggest users of surplus Douglas B-18 and C-58 Bolos was Mexico, and several cargo and passenger airlines used the type on their routes through the early 1970s. The type's rugged construction and ease of maintenance were appreciated in these backcountry operations. During early 1971, this well-used B-18B, with the nose radome for the ASW radar still in place, was returned to Tucson, Arizona. Carrying the Mexican civil registration XB-LAJ, it had been previously operated by Aero Service of Dalhart, Texas, as N67947 before heading south. The aircraft was transferred to the Pima Air Museum at Tucson but then moved to McChord AFB, Washington, in the belly of a C-5A where it has been restored to static display condition. Serial number 37-505 carries the rather derisive name B-18 Bummer sprayed on the nose, presumably relating to the ferry flight.

Defensive armament consisted of three Browning air-cooled .30 caliber machine guns—one in a nose turret driven by a hand-crank, a second in a similarly powered dorsal turret aft of wing, the third firing through a hatch in the lower aft fuselage. With a top speed of 220 miles per hour, a range of 1,030 miles, and a bomb load of 2,532 pounds, the

DB-1 met the Air Corps requirements, and the plane's similarity to the commercial transports already in production greatly reduced the near-inevitable problems attendant on phasing the craft into the Clover Field production lines.

Deliveries of B-18s began in early 1937 and on 23 February of that year, the first production aircraft (serial number 36-262) arrived at Wright Field where it was tested along with the DB-1. Other fields to receive early copies of the new bomber included Chanute Field, Illinois, the Aberdeen Proving Grounds in Maryland, and Colorado's Lowry Field. The next three planes off the production line were flown to Hamilton Field, California, for testing with the 7th Bombardment Group.

The initial production contract for the plane, Contract AC 8307, covered 113 planes with serial numbers 36-262 to 36-343, 36-431 to 36-446, 37-001 to 37-034, and was amended to include 37-051 (the DB-1 brought up to production standards and assigned a military serial). The new B-18s differed from the prototype in several ways including a redesigned nose which reduced overall length by seven inches and the addition of new equipment raised overall weight by 1,000 pounds. The bomber was also given the rather strange name of Bolo.

Not an attractive aircraft, the Bolo was assigned to the 5th Bombardment Group, Luke Field, Oahu, Territory of Hawaii; the 19th Bombardment Group and 38th Reconnaissance Squadron, Mitchel Field, New York; and the 21st Reconnaissance Squadron, Langley Field, Virginia.

The B-18's arrangement of nose gunner and bombardier was one of the design's weakest points; the forward fuselage was far too cramped to make it either comfortable or efficient when both men were at their positions. Douglas reworked their stations, the bombardier and gunner trading places. The upper position was moved forward, and the nose was extended into a blunt point to make room for the bomb sight. A ball-and-socket mount was installed in the lower position for the .30 caliber weapon.

The first B-18s used Wright R-1820-45 radials of 930 horsepower each. These were replaced by R-1820-53s of 1,000 horsepower each and fitted with full-feathering hydromatic propellers on the later B-18A. The Air Corps ordered 217 B-18As at a unit cost of $65,800. Contract AC 9977 covered serial numbers 37-458 to 37-634, 38-585 to 38-609, and 39-12 to 39-26, and the first B-18A took to the air on 15 April 1938.

By 1938, many European nations were eagerly looking toward America for

additional arms with which to face the growing threat of Hitler's Germany. A British delegation visited the Douglas factory and examined a Bolo but found the type to be underpowered with poor performance and armament. The British were quoted a unit price of $109,000 on a 200 plane order, and production would require fifty-eight weeks. This was unacceptable, and the British bought the cross-town rival, Lockheed's Model 14 Hudson. Douglas did, however, sell twenty of the aircraft to the Royal Canadian Air Force (RCAF), which called them Digby Mk. Is.

The Air Corps quickly realized that the Bolo was basically a failure, and large orders were placed with Boeing for the superb Flying Fortress. However, on 7 December 1941, Bolos were in service with the 5th and 11th Bombardment Groups at Hickam Field, Oahu, Territory of Hawaii, while a dozen Bolos were with the 27th and 28th bombardment groups in the Philippines. The Japanese sneak attack destroyed a large

number of Hickam's B-18s on the ground, but the B-18s in the Philippines began to operate at night as transports, flying parts and ammunition for the 19th Bombardment Group's surviving Flying Fortresses. At least three of the Bolos ran the daunting gauntlet to Australia, arriving at Darwin in the Northern territory where they were loaded with .50 caliber ammunition and sent back north.

The Bolo's combat career wasn't limited entirely to the Philippines, and the type was used for antisubmarine patrols on the East Coast and Canal Zone, and one Bolo actually sank a German U-boat in a determined attack. Other Bolos served as transports and were redesignated as C-58s after all combat equipment was stripped from the airframe. Also, eighteen B-18AMs and twenty-two B-18Ms were created by removal of bomb-carrying gear and the planes served as bomber-crew trainers.

In order to combat the U-boat threat, 122 B-18As were modified for antisubmarine warfare (ASW) use as B-18Bs, their patrols

Very well-worn B-18B N66267 had been operated for many years by Roberts Company, Boise, Idaho, as a large-acreage sprayer and may also have been used as an aerial fire fighter since the faint tanker number of 18D can be seen on the fabric-covered rudder. When photographed at Falcon Field, Arizona, during 1968, the aircraft was in long-term storage and was eventually transferred to the Pima Air Museum where it remains on display. N66267 (serial number 38-593) retained its ASW radome through its career and, besides the spraying gear, seems to have been little modified; the glass and ball socket for the .30 caliber machine gun are still in place below the radome. On a good day, the B-18 had a top speed of about 215 miles per hour.

eventually covering much of the Caribbean and the Gulf of Mexico. The radar and magnetic-detection gear made them particularly suitable for night missions, the

55

Arizona seemed to be the elephant's graveyard for Bolos during the 1960s. B-18A N56847 is seen in less than desirable condition at Tucson during May 1969. Surrounded by doomed A-26 Invaders, Constellations, and other vintage aircraft destined for the scrap heap, the old Bolo survived them all: serial number 37-469 is proudly displayed in magnificent condition at the US Air Force (USAF) Museum in Dayton, Ohio.

time when U-boats came to the surface to recharge their batteries and clear stale air out of their compartments. ASW radar was still in its infancy and contacts were both infrequent and undependable. Although depth charges were usually carried, trials were also undertaken with underwing rockets.

Early in 1942, one Bolo crew had a particularly interesting flight: Capt. N. D. Meadowcroft and his crew from the 90th Bombardment Squadron launched from Zandry Field, Surinam, to check out a reported submarine sighting. Searching the Caribbean 4,000 feet below their Bolo, the men spotted a dark shape, moving slowly beneath the surface. Setting up for an attack, Meadowcroft pushed his portly bomber over and dove on the target. Four depth charges plunged into the water in a perfect pattern, bracketing the ominous object—and as the crew watched, the weapons blew up an unfortunate whale! Upon their return, the briefing officer who had sent them out solemnly pinned up photographs of a German U-boat side-by-side with a whale and painstakingly pointed out the differences to the red-faced crew.

Meadowcroft and his men had also been one of at least three Bolo crews to acquire first-hand experience in another ability of their elderly machines. Forced down at sea when one engine gave up the ghost, the eight fliers scrambled out of their plane as it

Certainly the best known of all surviving B-23 Dragons, N747M has been a West Coast fixture for many years. Seen on 7 September 1975, the Dragon wears an attractive blue and white scheme with very appropriate artwork on the huge vertical tail. Note the airstair door and extended nose section common to the Pan American conversions. When originally surplused, serial number 39-033 was registered as N747 to Howard Hughes and was sold to Rexall Drugs in 1950.

Dragon N747M seen at the 190 Reno Air Races illustrates its current condition of gleaming polished aluminum skin and early Army Air Corps markings. For a time, this plane was loaned to the Douglas Historical Foundation where it was hoped it would become a permanent flying exhibit with their DC-2. But when owner Ed Daly (who also owned World Airways) died, the aircraft was put up for sale by the company and purchased by Mike Bogue and partners, who regularly attended air shows in the classic. This view also shows the many additional windows to advantage.

bobbed about in the Caribbean. A Dutch patrol boat from the naval base at Surinam eventually picked them up but their B-18 refused to sink and five days later it was towed back by a tug, washed down, and put in a hangar to serve as a parts supply for the 99th's other Bolos.

As newer aircraft, such as the Consolidated B-24 Liberator, became available for the ASW mission, the Bolos

were pulled from service and usually were used as trainers or transports. After the war, there was no use for the type and the survivors were put up for sale.

Oddly, the surplus Bolos found a ready civilian market since the planes had the same good flying characteristics as the DC-2 and DC-3, but their deeper fuselage could be used for hauling larger loads. Some Bolos were fitted with large cargo doors in the sides of their fuselages, others were fitted out as crop sprayers, while at least one became a fire bomber with Hawkins & Powers in Greybull, Wyoming. At least three Mexican airlines made extensive use of surplus Bolos over the years. As time went by, however, the few B-18s left flying were gradually grounded, and the last of the type to fly was the Hawkins & Powers fire bomber that was made airworthy and flown to a US Air Force (USAF) base for static display in the early 1980s. Fortunately, a few more examples survive in museums to illustrate an interesting period in American aeronautical history.

The next bomber to come from the Clover Field factory was as elegant as the

Bolo was bulky. Both Douglas and the Air Corps realized early on that the B-18 was, at best, a stopgap that could not compete in the rapidly developing European arena of aerial warfare. Douglas wanted to create an improved Bolo that would feature more powerful engines and use the stronger wings from the DC-3 transport. Wright had developed the new R-2600 double-row radial engine that could pump out 1,600 horsepower in its early -2 version, and the engine promised good growth potential. Douglas and the Air Corps debated on the aircraft and what finally emerged had little in common with the B-18.

The method of ordering the new aircraft was rather unorthodox. The Air Corps converted an order for thirty-eight B-18As that had already been purchased to an equal number of the new design. At this point in history, the military would usually order prototype aircraft (with an X before the designation), and these would be tested to make sure the design was appropriate for production. The experimental planes would usually be followed by an order for thirteen service test aircraft (with a Y before the

58

designation), and these machines would be handed out to operational units for testing by service pilots. The new plane was unique in that it was simply designated B-23: There were no XB-23s or YB-23s for testing.

The new B-23 rolled out of its hangar during July 1939 and, in its gleaming aluminum finish, the bomber was a study in Art Deco design with its very large vertical tail and gracefully swept-back DC-3 wings. Not looking anything like the Bolo, the B-23 had a sleek, purposeful fuselage and tightly cowled R-2600 radials. Even the landing gear was enclosed in streamlined fairings that added a few more miles per hour to the top speed (a variation of these units would be fitted to "performance" DC-3 modifications after the war). With its surface finish unblemished except for national insignia and the colorful red, white, and blue rudder stripes of the time, the B-23 *looked* like the high-performance aircraft that the Air Corps desired.

Looks and reality are often two different things and the B-23, which was given the name Dragon, was to remain a limited production aircraft. First flown on 27 July 1939, the first B-23 (serial number 39-27) proved to be fairly slippery in the air. When the test crew shoved the throttles all the way forward, they achieved over 280 miles per hour—not a bad speed and well over sixty miles per hour faster than the best the Bolo could offer. With large foreign orders pouring in, American aviation manufacturers quickly began to change as lessons of early aerial combat over Europe were learned and these changes were to lead to advanced, combat capable aircraft that would quickly leave the B-23 behind.

One of the major flaws with the B-23 design was the armament: One .30 caliber Browning was fitted in a ball-and-socket mount in the nose; a second similar weapon was carried in the fuselage to be fired out of side hatches; a third .30 caliber could be fired

The Dragon taxis by the photographer at Chino, California, during September 1978. It is easy to see why Howard Hughes was attracted to the Dragon since the aircraft, with its sleek Art Deco design, almost looked like one of his stylized air racers.

from a ventral hatch; and a .50 caliber Browning was mounted in the aft fuselage to be fired by a prone gunner. This weapon was fitted in a plexiglass cone that opened like a clamshell when the weapon was used. All of these guns were "man powered" and the B-23 did not really have the capability of carrying a power turret (although Emerson did use a B-23 during the war as a test bed for some of its turret designs).

The bomb bay of the Dragon could hold up to 2,000 pounds of bombs but the plane also had provisions to carry a large Fairchild aerial camera mounted in the left side of the

Dragon N1755 was photographed at Panama City, Panama, on 20 June 1973, where the B-23 had been impounded following an abortive 1971 drug flight. Serial number 39-062 was originally flown by General Electric as N33310 before going through several other owners. The aircraft was eventually cut up for scrap during the late 1970s.

added, the B-23 (now designated UC-67) became a very comfortable way to travel and many of the planes were obtained by officers of general rank and jealously guarded as almost personal possessions.

At the end of the war, surviving B-23 and UC-67 airframes were put up for surplus sale. Virtually every example was purchased, and it is doubtful whether any B-23 went to the smelter. The aircraft were extremely popular with the bigger corporations, and General Electric alone purchased five for executive conversion (N33310, N33311, N45361, N56249, and N61666), while eccentric billionaire Howard Hughes also purchased quite a few—the plane apparently being one of his all-time favorites. The engineering department of Pan American World Airways carried out a number of conversions and most of their aircraft were fitted with a longer streamlined metal nose that probably helped boost the top speed a bit. The executive Dragons were a very classy way to travel during the Fabulous Fifties.

By the time executive business jets, such as the Lear, were becoming available, the Dragon was getting a bit long in the tooth, and most of the aircraft became second- and third-line equipment, a few even being destroyed in drug smuggling flights. Several of the civilian examples, however, have found their way into the USAF Museum and are distributed to various bases around the country. As of this writing, two Dragons remain airworthy while another two are under restoration to flying status.

The only other Dragon currently airworthy is N777LW, which was photographed at Loma Rica Airport, Grass Valley, California, during September 1968. Serial number 39-063 was originally converted as N47994 for Esso Shipping and is now owned by Robert Schlaefli, Moses Lake, Washington.

62

Previous page
Capts. Jim Mars and Brad Kenyon pilot Dakota 12938 over a California lake. The final Canadian Forces Dakotas were jointly operated by No. 402 "City of Winnipeg" Squadron and the Instrument Check Pilot School at CFB Winnipeg.

Dakota 12938 with the gear down. Although the FAA has tried a number of ploys over the years to ground the gracefully aging Gooney fleet, the aircraft's immense strength makes it difficult for the bureaucrats to find sufficient reason for grounding.

Normandy One—Dakota 12944—was finished in approximate No. 437 Squadron markings used during 1944 in Europe. Dakota 12944 was used in the "West Flight into History"—departing CFB Winnipeg to visit appropriate airfields in Canada's west. The aircraft is seen over scenic Vancouver Island during April 1989, as the plane heads for CFB Comox.

As Normandy One headed for nearby Victoria and another visit, several warbirds escorted the Dakota, including this restored North American T-28 Trojan.

On 31 March 1989, the sun set on Dakota operations with the Canadian Forces as the aircraft were mustered out of service in a two-day ceremony.

Under a sullen sky, the Dakota fleet was arranged for the retirement ceremony—which was attended by many people who had flown and worked on the craft during the Dakota's nearly five decades of Canadian service.

Several of the Dakotas had not flown in some time, but the aircraft were kept carefully stored in case they would be needed. The Dakota fleet even had a war assignment: If a conflict were to break out, the Dakotas would be used for second-line aerial movement of personnel and cargo.

Fondly nicknamed Pinocchio, *Dakota 12959 had been fitted with an F-104 radome for radar training when the type was still on active service in Canada. This aircraft, along with Normandy One and Burma One, has been retained for preservation in Canada.*

Turbine Goonies

Over the years a number of modifications have been made to the DC-3 to bring the craft into the jet age. Finally, one has been found that works.

During World War II, Britain was a major developer of jet power, beginning with Frank (later Sir Frank) Whittle and progressing to a number of manufacturers that put the country in the forefront of jet development—to the point where the United States had to borrow powerplants from the British to power the Bell P-59 Airacomet and Lockheed P-80 Shooting Star. During the war, Britain developed the de Havilland Vampire and the Gloster Meteor. Unfortunately, these aircraft were not pitted against the might of the fading Luftwaffe, but Meteors did manage to destroy some of the thousands of dreaded V-1 buzz bombs that were launched by a desperate Hitler against the United Kingdom.

These early jets consumed prodigious amounts of fuel, limiting the range of the early fighters and making the engine, at that point, really only practical for point-defense fighters. British scientists, however, reasoned

The second Jack Conroy DC-3 modification involved taking one of just four Super DC-3s built and adding turbines. Once again, the hulk of former United Viscount N7441 was called upon to shed its two remaining engines. The Super Turbo-Three is seen taxiing for takeoff during its unveiling "first" flight for the press at Santa Barbara during May 1974.

that the jet could be combined with a geared propeller to produce a turboprop engine that would be more fuel-efficient and would offer a lower speed than a pure jet. British manufacturers knew that the war was coming to an end and they also realized the United States had gained the upper hand in transport aircraft with the wartime Douglas C-54 Skymaster and Lockheed C-69 Constellation. These planes were powered by conventional reciprocating engines and the British felt that a major coup would be obtained by developing a postwar airliner with turboprop power.

In 1949, two competing British engine builders each obtained a Dakota to modify to turboprop power. Armstrong Siddeley had developed a compact turbine named Mamba, and two such engines were fitted in Dakota KJ839 for testing. The turboprops offered more power, yet were much lighter than the Wright radials. Engineers had to move the motor mounts and nacelles farther forward to compensate for the lost weight. Rolls-Royce obtained Dakota KJ829 and fitted the craft with their new Dart turboprops. Both companies extensively flight-tested the new engines. The Dart went on to enjoy amazing success, but the Mamba became a rather limited production engine—Fairey used a combined powerplant, called the Double Mamba in the equally curious Gannett carrier-based ASW craft.

In order to obtain turboprop experience, British European Airways (BEA, today's British Airways) decided to fit two Dakotas with Darts for proving trials. These aircraft were painted in full BEA markings and were used for route-proving and passenger appeal. Some historians have incorrectly assumed that BEA wanted a fleet of turboprop Goonies but this was far from the truth, since the aircraft were not pressurized and could not operate at altitudes that made the turboprops more efficient. The Dart would, however, power the new generation of pressurized Vickers Viscount transports that would be extremely successful. The Dart-Dakotas helped pave the way.

After these worthwhile experiments, little was thought about DC-3 turboprops until the 1960s when a number of interesting ideas were created in the ever-fertile mind of John "call me Jack" M. Conroy. In the early 1960s, Conroy came up with the idea of taking a Boeing 377 or C-97 airframe and expanding the fuselage to gigantic proportions in order to facilitate the carriage of very outsized cargo such as missiles or fuselage sections of the new generation of "jumbo" airliner that was being predicted by Boeing and other companies.

Although Conroy's vision was oft-ridiculed, he had plenty of background. As an ANG pilot, Conroy had set a cross-country speed record in a California ANG

Conroy Turbo-Three N4700C on the ramp at Santa Barbara displays the long cowlings required to balance the lighter weight of the Rolls-Royce Dart turboprop engines. For safety, the propellers could not be located abeam the cockpit. Conroy had increased fuel capacity on 00C from 822 to 1,922 gallons and added a fuel dump system. A complete lack of orders led to the dropping of the Turbo-Three program, but 00C would be back.

Sabre by having breakfast in Los Angeles, lunch in New York, and dinner in Los Angeles—all in the same day. Conroy also had lots of friends in the aviation industry. When he was working for Hughes Aircraft in Culver City, California, he would commute to work by simply hopping in an ANG Sabre at Van Nuys and flying the twenty miles to the field at Culver City. Try that today!

After several of his Boeing conversions were successfully built (the first being dubbed the *Pregnant Guppy*—its test flight from Van Nuys Airport caused local bureaucrats to close down the Ventura Freeway over which

Airborne over Santa Barbara, DC-3S N156WC was accompanied by N666DG, which hauled the press and served as a chase aircraft. N666DG was originally built as DC-3-208A NC21748 for American Airlines and was delivered on 25 February 1939. It was built with Cyclones but was converted to Twin Wasps during 1949. The plane was last seen operating out of Miami and the differences between the two types can clearly be seen.

the aircraft would pass for "safety"—stupidity on the bureaucrats' part but great for publicity), Conroy turned his mind to converting DC-3s to turboprop power. Much had happened since those 1949 experiments but Conroy was still way ahead of the time—today rebuilding and reengining of older airliners is fairly common and profitable.

For his first Gooney project, Conroy decided to strip a former United Airlines Vickers Viscount (Dart engines—remember?) that was being phased out of service and install two of said engines on a Gooney. This left two more engines on the Viscount for either another turboprop Gooney or for recycling as spares. Accordingly, a Viscount was purchased for engines (they were going for scrap value since no one wanted the Viscounts) and C-53

serial number 41-20133 was purchased for conversion. This aircraft had gone through several owners after the military, including TWA, and Conroy was able to purchase the bird at a reasonable price and begin conversion at Goleta, California.

United Viscount N7441 began losing engines to the project, which was named the Turbo-Three and registered N4700C, during 1968 at the Santa Barbara Airport. The Viscount was fitted with 1,650 shaft horsepower Darts and the FAA soon began rearing its ugly head. When fully loaded, the aircraft would be over the standard DC-3's max weight so the FAA demanded heavier landing gear and a fuel dump system. Conroy's workers ripped the plane apart, repairing where necessary and adding new systems such as increasing total fuel from 822

N4700C eventually returned in the form of N23SA, the Tri-Turbo-Three. One of the main reasons that the original airliner was built was to get rid of the inefficient tri-motors then in service, so it is interesting to see what happened four decades after the DC-3's birth. The new cowlings for the Pratt & Whitney Canada PT-6 turbines are much cleaner than earlier Conroy experiments, and the Hartzell five-blade props were also a big improvement. Finished in a pseudo-Coast Guard color scheme, the Tri-Turbo-Three was extensively promoted, but the plane just could not find the orders that were needed to get the conversion program going. The plane was eventually sold to Polair and operated very successfully in the Arctic Circle for quite a few seasons before being flown to Mojave in late 1991 for scrapping.

to 1,922 gallons. Conroy decided to initially derate the Darts to 1,350 shaft horsepower each to get by some of the FAA rules, although he later hoped to get the horsepower back to its standard rating. The nacelles were brought forward to get the four-blade propellers past the crew compartment. The first flight of the Turbo-Three was made on 13 May 1969. A number of test hours were flown before the aircraft headed across the pond to attend the Paris air show. An intensive sales program was mounted, but even though the aircraft's performance was impressive (cruising at 215 miles per hour at a 32,000 pound weight with a range of 2,250 miles), no one bought.

Conroy had promised that conversion could be done in thirty days but, at that time point, purchasers of such aircraft had newer planes on their minds. Conroy was ahead of his time. Also, the FAA and Douglas took a very dim view of the plane because it combined an old airframe with old turboprops, and the bureaucrats made certification of the Turbo-Three an impossibility. The aircraft came back to Santa Barbara, but Conroy's DC-3 dreams were only just beginning.

Reorganizing as Specialized Aircraft Corporation, Conroy and the owner of the third production Super DC-3 (N16012, N5425, and N111SA) put their heads together and came up with the idea that what the Super Gooney really needed was turboprop power. Accordingly, the aircraft was flown to Santa Barbara (at the time, the plane was owned by Western Company of North America) during 1975, and modifications were begun to convert the aircraft to turboprop power. Since the DC-3S already had a stretched fuselage, the new (and crude) fiberglass nacelles extended to behind the cockpit. Many other modifications were made besides fitting the Dart 510s of 1,742 shaft horsepower each, and included additional fuel and dumps for the same.

Named the Super Turbo-Three, the FAA gave the rather unattractive plane a Supplemental Type Certificate (STC) for one time use. The particular aircraft was one of the trio that had served with Capital Airlines as N16012, and it made its first flight with the new engines during May 1974.

It is difficult to exactly define what market Conroy and the owner had in mind

Warren Basler and one of his BT-67 aircraft—the most successful of any Gooney Bird major modification.

since the Super DC-3 was a limited production aircraft and, at the time, most were still in military service. The aircraft did quite a bit of flight testing but was either finally sold or transferred to Pilgrim Airlines where the registration N156PM was assigned but never taken up. The aircraft was abandoned at New London, Connecticut, and was finally scrapped.

Not to be discouraged, Conroy went back to the Turbo-Three which had been languishing at the field and began plans for a "new" aircraft. Conroy wanted to create a high-tech DC-3, junking the old Darts in favor of new Pratt & Whitney Canada PT6A-45 turboprops. This time, however, he wanted to make the Gooney into a tri-motor! Although this went against the original Douglas-American Airlines philosophy that

wanted to see an end to tri-motors, Conroy rationalized that such a plane would have Third World military appeal. N4700C had its registration changed to N23SA, the airframe was completely stripped, and the new engines were added in high-tech nacelles along with five-blade Hartzell propellers. In flight, the center engine could be turned off for operations such as extended search and rescue or maritime patrol.

Its first flight was on 2 November 1977 and the aircraft was flown to several major air shows, including Farnborough. Once again, however, the Tri-Turbo-Three, finished in a "sort of" Coast Guard scheme, failed to find a buyer. Named *Spirit of Hope*, reflecting on the sad fact that Conroy had been diagnosed with fatal cancer, the aircraft languished since the FAA and Douglas were strictly opposed

BT-67 N8059P is seen over an Oshkosh cloud deck and piloted by Gene Smith and Bob Clark. The composite cowlings housing the turboprops have been designed to contribute to the aircraft's overall lift.

to seeing the modification having any success. The plane was sold to Polair Incorporated on 20 August 1979 and painted in an attractive black and yellow scheme. The aircraft was extensively operated on skis in the arctic where the author, who obtained the craft's logs, surmises that it was used for Central Intelligence Agency (CIA) operations as well as a number of other extremely odd flights.

The old bird was a real performer but, while "wintering" at Santa Barbara, a

Eight DC-3s can be accommodated in the modern 75,000 square foot factory. The DC-3s come from a wide variety of sources, and if this hangar could talk, the tales would fill a book.

more orders came in—including two from the US Forest Service. Also, more foreign air forces were showing interest and several deals have been worked out with Latin American nations.

With the BT-67, the future looks bright for Gooney Birds operating a long, long time. The company reworks all Goonies going through their shop to the same zero-life standard. The entire airframe is strengthened, the cockpit is made more pilot friendly, and any combination of avionics can be fitted. With all possible options, a BT-67 will cost approximately $3.7 million.

Interesting options include new outer-wing fuel tanks that can increase capacity from fifty to 100 percent. A standard wing cuff helps improve stall behavior. The composite engine nacelle has been designed to provide lift—certainly something the radial's cowling did not do! In an all-cargo mode, the cabin can carry up to five LD3 containers.

Even at the fully-optioned price, the BT-67 is much less expensive than comparable new aircraft. Warren Basler intends to find new customers and convert more Goonies as the success of the BT-67 convinces customers that "the only replacement for a DC-3 is another DC-3."

BT-67 gunship for the air force of El Salvador. Note that the majority of windows are of the original type. In this configuration, the Gooney carries three side-mounted Browning .50 caliber air-cooled machine guns and lots of ammunition. The overwing exhausts make the turboprop conversion a less tempting target for shoulder-launched heat-seeking missiles.

The cockpit of N8059P features over $250,000 of advanced avionics. Even the old control yokes have been replaced with more modern units.

Previous page
Tim Braidy displays the fine lines of the C-41
over a San Francisco fog bank. The C-41 was
the first military Gooney, and over 10,000
more follow. Gen. Dwight D. Eisenhower
quite correctly described the C-47 as one of
the ten reasons the Allies won World War II,
and it is amazing that the first military
Gooney is still intact and flying.

One of the most popular sights in San
Francisco is the Golden Gate Bridge and
N97H is seen giving its passengers a close
look at the structure. Both the DC-3 and the
Golden Gate were created during the Art
Deco era, and both became design classics.

Out to Pasture

As the most numerous of all passenger and cargo aircraft, it is not surprising that abandoned or wrecked Gooney Bird hulks can be found in almost every part of the globe.

Any enthusiast of vintage and veteran aircraft that gets a chance to travel is always on the lookout for strange and unusual planes that may be parked in the weeds behind a hangar at remote airfields. There really is no telling what one can find since it is a big world, but the traveler can readily be assured of stumbling upon the hulk of a Gooney Bird somewhere on his or her journeys.

I can't really recall the first abandoned Gooney Bird that I chanced upon as a child, but I do have a box camera photo of a couple of wingless hulks sitting on a remote Oklahoma airfield some time during the early 1960s. As my aviation activities became more organized, I fondly recall unscrewing both the military and factory identification plates from C-53 serial number 41-20089, which was being scrapped at Whiteman Airpark in

For US military Gooney Birds, Davis-Monthan AFB, Tucson, Arizona, became an elephant's graveyard. The majority of surviving airframes have been stored at one time or another at the huge facility. Some have been scrapped, some sent to foreign air forces, and some recycled and sold to civilian operators. Photographed during August 1970, this Vietnam War–era camouflaged Gooney (Road Runner Airlines) stands in stark contrast to the bare metal veterans in the background.

Southern California during the mid-1960s. (Yes, I still have them—stuffed away in my aviation memorabilia file.)

Since that time, I have been fortunate to travel fairly extensively and have managed to see and photograph many derelict or wrecked Gooney Birds in diverse locations. When traveling in Third World countries, one must always remember that cameras are usually frowned upon by the locals, and care has to be exercised in taking photos. In fact, one enthusiast that I met let his zeal for aircraft get a bit out of hand and was arrested and imprisoned in Greece for taking photos of landing military aircraft while he was *outside* the perimeter of the base.

I have had occasional run-ins with authorities who did not want aircraft photographed. One memorable image, which would have been great in this chapter, was a row of about two dozen wingless Gooney Birds parked shoulder to shoulder on a hill in Manila. They were painted in a wide range of camouflage colors but, try as I might, my escort would not let the hulks be photographed. I think he was actually more embarrassed than anything else since a number of Philippine homeless was residing in the hulks.

In Central America, I had a sixteen-year-old soldier point an M16 in my face after photographing a hulk. Fortunately, I could see that the weapon was unloaded. In Saigon,

I recall rows of Gooney Birds neatly parked during the fall of South Vietnam. The invading North Vietnamese knew better than to shell the packed airfield since these planes could be pressed into service once final victory had been achieved. Even though this situation was chaotic, no photos were allowed.

Even though the DC-3 and C-47 series of aircraft is one of the toughest ever designed and built, time does take its toll and each year we will see fewer and fewer of these classics take to the air. Certain parts are becoming difficult to obtain, while inspections and repairs are increasing in cost. Also, the radial engines are becoming tired as they are rebuilt over and over. Avgas is another problem since it is becoming difficult to obtain in many parts of the world.

The Gooney Bird has been one of the most recycled aircraft of all time. Of the hundreds of airframes that passed through the vast acreage of Davis-Monthan AFB over the years, many have been rebuilt to fly again. In fact, many of the aircraft have been stored several times at the base during their long lives.

All good things, however, do come to an end, so if you are an enthusiast of one of the finest Douglas aircraft ever built, take some time out when you next see a Gooney Bird. Take some photos, talk to the pilots, and, if at all possible, go for a ride!

Certainly one of the most attractively displayed preserved Gooney Birds, this aircraft was originally built as serial number 43-48189 for the USAAF and delivered on 24 July 1944, but immediately transferred to the RAF as Dakota Mk. III KG773. The plane operated with the RAF until March 1947 when it was sold to Scottish Aviation, who specialized in converting military transports to civil use. Registered as G-AKLL, the plane was sold to Hornton Airways Limited and was heavily involved in the Berlin Airlift, flying well over one hundred missions during that tense period in 1948. In 1950, the aircraft went to Iberia in Spain as EC-AEU and operated with that airline for sixteen years before going to the Spanish air force. Finally withdrawn from use in 1977, the aircraft was sold to an American company and registered N8041A but never delivered. Languishing at Barcelona, Spain, the aircraft was purchased by Air Classik, and registered D-CORA. During May 1980, the Dakota was placed on display in Stuttgart, Germany.

Mounted on pylons at the entrance to the State Fair in Oklahoma City, Oklahoma (with the prototype Aero Commander in the background), this aircraft was delivered to the USAAF as C-47A-15-DK serial number 42-92838 on 5 March 1944. The plane saw action with both the Eighth and Ninth air forces in Europe and probably participated in the D-day invasion. Returned to the States and placed in storage, the aircraft was sold surplus on 31 October 1945 as NC65162. During its civil life, the aircraft had only one owner—the Kerr McGee Oil Industry Incorporated. The company donated the plane to the Fair in 1977.

Photographed on 9 January 1990, the remains of N163E are seen residing in an aviation junkyard at El Mirage, California. Originally built as serial number 42-15877 for the USAAF, the aircraft was sold to Northwest Airlines in March 1945 as NC33331. Over the years, the aircraft went through several owners and registration changes before becoming N163E with Escort Air Taxis of Las Vegas, Nevada, in 1976. The plane went through several other owners before being damaged in a taxiing accident at Burbank, California, on 5 December 1982, and withdrawn from further use.

During the 1960s and early 1970s, Ryan Field, near Tucson, Arizona, was a mecca for down-and-out Gooney Birds. A civilian company on the field would buy the aircraft during surplus sales at Davis-Monthan and transport the planes to then-remote Ryan where they were usually parted out, but some were restored to flying condition for civil operators. Serial number 42-23336 was flown by the Ninth Air Force during 1945 in Europe as Y9-T with the name Red Dog. Stored at Davis-Monthan in 1961, the plane was sold shortly after to Aero American Corporation as N87639. The plane apparently did not enjoy much of a civilian life before being taken to Ryan for stripping where it was photographed on 6 April 1968.

Serial number 43-48875 was delivered to the USAAF during September 1944 and was later converted to a C-47E, one of eight such conversions undertaken by Pan American for airways checks. The main part of the conversion was the installation of two Pratt & Whitney R-2000-4 radials of 1,290 horsepower each. This hulk was given the registration N87656 when it was purchased as surplus by Aero American Corporation but it is doubtful that the aircraft ever flew with the registration. Completely gutted of anything usable, including the cargo door, the fuselage is seen at Ryan Field on 6 April 1968.

Eighty-one C-47A-DLs ordered by the USAAF were transferred to the US Navy before delivery and were later supplemented by 157 C-47A-DKs. All aircraft received BuNos and were designated R4D-5s (changed to C-74H in 1962 under the new triservice designation system). This particular example, BuNo 17192, was delivered to the Naval Air Transport Service on 14 April 1944 and went on to fly with a number of squadrons during the war including VR-1, VRS-1, and VRF-1 before being placed into storage at NAS Litchfield Park, Arizona, during mid-1947. Removed from storage and brought back to flying status, the aircraft was assigned to NAS Chase Field before being placed into storage at Davis-Monthan AFB in 1961. This 1967 view shows the aircraft with the ominous "strike" painted on the nose (meaning the decision had been made to scrap the aircraft) and the wings removed.

This C-47 was delivered to the USAAF as serial number 42-93791 and was eventually assigned to the South Carolina Air National Guard (ANG) in May 1961. During 1968, the aircraft was heavily damaged in a windstorm and, as this 13 April 1968 view illustrates, the decision was made to strip the airframe of useful parts and then scrap the remainder. During the 1950s and 1960s, C-47s were a staple item of virtually every ANG unit. The photo was taken at McEntire.

Hawaiian Airlines was a long-time operator of the DC-3 before retiring its fleet during 1966 in favor of newer equipment. The stored aircraft are seen at Honolulu awaiting a new buyer. N95469 was originally delivered as R4D-3 BuNo 06996 to the US Navy on 10 September 1942 and then went to Hawaiian after being surplused. Following sale by Hawaiian, N95469 went through several owners before being canceled from the register during 1971. Its ultimate fate is unknown.

During the 1950s and 1960s, both the Navy and Air Force marked many of their aircraft in brilliant hues of DaGlo paint and these two newly arrived Gooney Birds at Davis-Monthan on 29 December 1962 are no exception. The aircraft in the foreground is EC-47D serial number 44-76643, which was delivered to the USAAF during March 1945. By the time the photo was taken, the plane was serving with the USAF Communications Service. After a few years in storage, the aircraft was made flyable and flown to South Vietnam for service with the South Vietnamese air force. The EC-47D was destroyed at Ton Son Nhut Air Base, Saigon, on 20 February 1968, by enemy shellfire.

Latin America is a great hunting ground for Gooney Bird hulks. This Fuerza Aerea Hondurena (FAH) craft is seen minus wings and engines at Tegucigalpa during December 1982. FAH-307 was delivered on 17 June 1968 to the FAH after having seen service with the USAF's 605th Air Commando Squadron. Like many other Gooneys in this condition, there is always a chance that the aircraft will be once again made flyable.

Two Yugoslavian workmen take great exception as the hulk of a Yugoslavian air force (Jugoslovenske Ratno Vazduhplovstvo) C-47 is photographed. Originally receiving Russian-built Li-2s supplied by the Soviets, the Yugoslavians also received C-47s from France and the United States. The planes were phased out of service and replaced by AN-26s during 1976. Some of the Gooneys were sold surplus in the States during 1980.

A field full of retired French Armee de l'Air C-47s is seen during June 1969. Serial number 42-24166 was originally delivered to the RAF as FL510 on 9 August 1943. In 1956, the plane was sold to Eagle Aircraft Services as G-AOYE. In 1957, it was again sold, this time to the Armee de l'Air. Surplused in 1971, the Gooney went to Canada as CF-POY with Laurentian Air Service and has remained operational with several owners since then.

Index